THE GREAT EMOJI QUIZBOOK

THE GREAT EMOJI QUIZBOOK

200 emoji puzzles to put a smiley on your face

MARTIN TOSELAND

CASSELL ILLUSTRATED

An Hachette UK Company
www.hachette.co.uk

First published in Great Britain in 2016
by Cassell, a division of
Octopus Publishing Group Ltd
Carmelite House
50 Victoria Embankment
London EC4Y 0DZ
www.octopusbooks.co.uk

Distributed in the US by
Hachette Book Group
1290 Avenue of the Americas
4th and 5th Floors
New York, NY 10020

Distributed in Canada by
Canadian Manda Group
664 Annette St.
Toronto, Ontario, Canada M6S 2C8

ISBN 978 1 84403 896 1

A CIP catalogue record for this book is
available from the British Library.

Printed and bound in China

10 9 8 7 6 5 4 3 2 1

Text: Martin Toseland
Additional material: Trevor Davies,
Francesca Leung, Tahmeed Zaki,
Caren Davies, Laura Cremer, Moya Koren,
Emily Rushgrove, Joe Cottington and
Hannah Knowles.

Editorial Director: Trevor Davies
Editorial Assistant: Francesca Leung
Designer: Eoghan O'Brien at Wide Open Studio
Production Controller: Sarah Kulasek-Boyd

CONTENTS

INTRODUCTION

How fluently can you speak emoji? Perhaps your vocabulary is quite limited; even a little unadventurous (I hesitate to use the word 'unemojinative')? A few smileys, the odd thumbs-up, swivel finger or unhappy face? You might venture as far as a cocktail glass and a party hat? But did you know there are over 1,100 characters to choose from? It turns out you can describe just about anything using these little symbols.

In *The Great Emoji Quizbook*, you'll be challenged to identify everything from quotes in classic literature, the plots of entire novels, vintage sporting moments, song lyrics, events in world history, great speeches, Shakespeare (yes, even he's not immune from 'emojification' – sorry), to biographies of the great and the good, all 'written' in Japanese picture characters.

Because we carry our phones with us everywhere, emojis are rapidly becoming the shorthand language of the future. So, this is your chance to expand your language skills in ways that haven't been tested since archaeologists discovered etched pictures of strange-looking birds and oddly shaped sticks on the walls of the Pyramids. *The Great Emoji Quizbook* is here to test your emojination (can I get away with that one?) and expand your vocabulary.

LEVELS OF DIFFICULTY:

EASY   **MODERATE**   **DIFFICULT**

AN EMOJI HISTORY OF THE WORLD

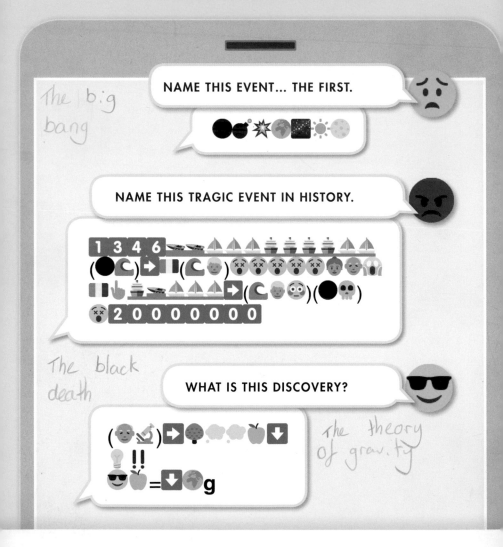

The big bang

NAME THIS EVENT... THE FIRST.

NAME THIS TRAGIC EVENT IN HISTORY.

The black death

WHAT IS THIS DISCOVERY?

The theory of gravity

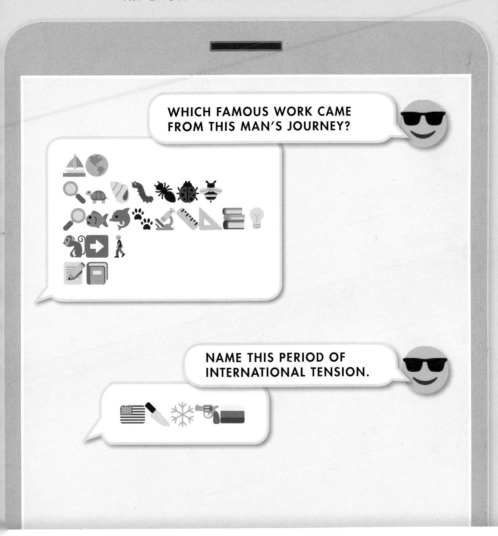

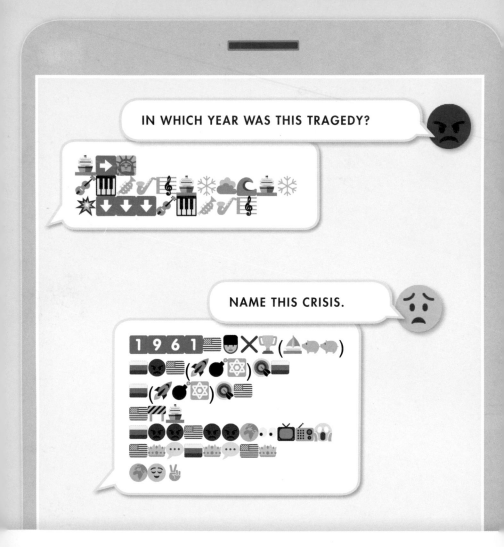

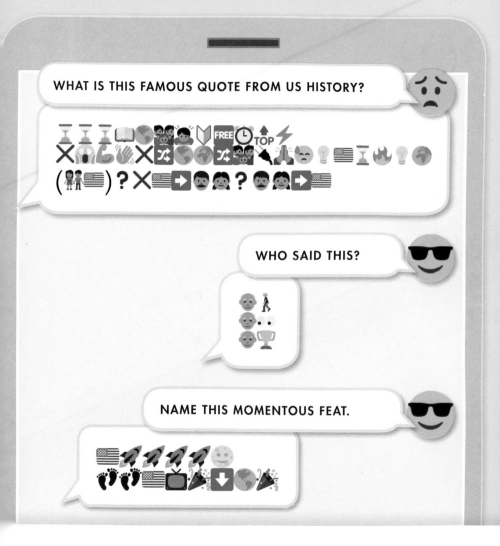

WHAT IS THIS FAMOUS QUOTE FROM US HISTORY?

WHO SAID THIS?

NAME THIS MOMENTOUS FEAT.

WHERE DID THIS EVENT TAKE PLACE?

NAME THE SHIPS THIS MAN CAPTAINED IN 1492.

🐙🇮🇹 1 4 5 1

👦➡️⚓

1 4 7 9 👦👰

👦➡️🏠🇪🇸

(🇪🇸👑)➡️👦💰➡️⛵

1 4 9 2 👦⛵🌍🧺☀️🇺🇸

👦⛵🇺🇸❌2

👦➡️🏠🇪🇸

1 5 0 6 👦💀

WHOSE JOURNEY WAS THIS?

WHO'S LIFE IS IT ANYWAY?

NAME THIS AMERICAN ICON?

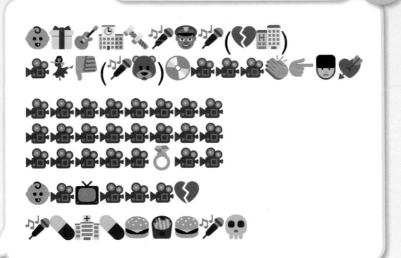

NAME THIS ACTRESS?

NAME THE SIX WOMEN IN THIS MAN'S LIFE?

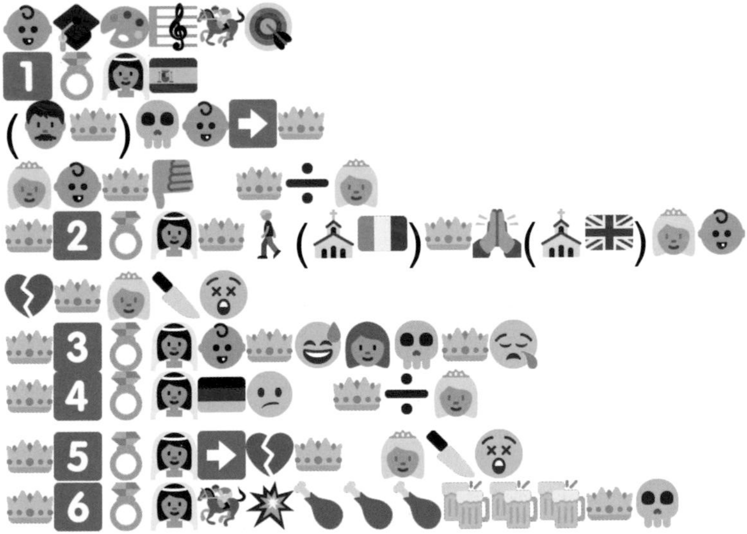

WHOSE LIFE IS IT ANYWAY?

WHICH LEADER IS THIS?

WHICH SINGER IS THIS?

WHERE WAS THIS INSPIRATIONAL LEADER IMPRISONED FOR 18 YEARS?

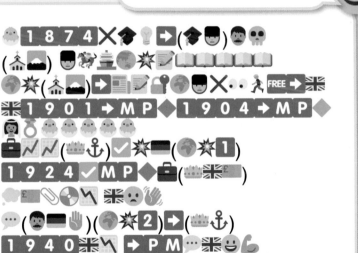

NAME THIS FAMOUS QUOTE FROM HIM?

WHO IS THIS WOMAN?

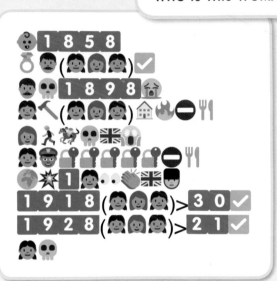

IN WHICH CENTURY WAS THIS GENIUS BORN?

WHOSE LIFE IS IT ANYWAY?

IN WHICH CENTURY WAS THIS SCIENTIST BORN?

HOW OLD WAS THIS WOMAN WHEN SHE DIED?

MOVIE STRINGS

MOVIE STRINGS

NAME THE FILM AND THE YEAR OF ITS RELEASE.

[Emoji puzzle]

NAME THIS CLASSIC 1970S FILM.

NAME THIS MOVIE FROM 2012.

MOVIE STRINGS

WHO DIRECTED THIS 1993 COMEDY?

(☀️🌥️⛈️🕯️👨🏾) 😠 🐭🐭🎬(📋👩🏾) 🎞️🐭🐭🚐❄️z z^z

🌥️🕕6😠🐭🐭🎬(📋👩)🎞️🐭🐭🚐❄️z z^z

🌥️🕐6(☀️🌥️⛈️☂️👨🏾) ❓❓❓z z^z

🌥️🕐6(☀️🌥️⛈️☂️🕯️👨🏾) 💬👨‍👩‍👧‍👦👫😐z z^z

🌥️🕐6↖️🕐z z^z

🌥️🕐6(☀️🌥️⛈️☂️👨🏾) 💕📦🚚💥💀z z^z

🌥️🕐6(☀️🌥️⛈️☂️🕯️👨🏾) 😄(📋👩)✖️z z^z

🌥️🕐6(☀️🌥️⛈️🕯️🐭) 💕(📋👩)✖️(☀️🌥️⛈️🕯️👨🏾) 🔪🎹

🔪💬🎚️🔪🎩⛄...💘

MOVIE STRINGS

WHICH DISNEY FILM IS THIS ADAPTATION?

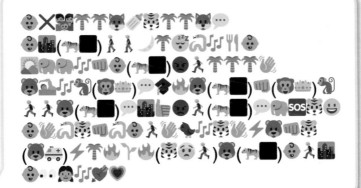

NAME THIS HORROR MOVIE RELEASED IN 1981.

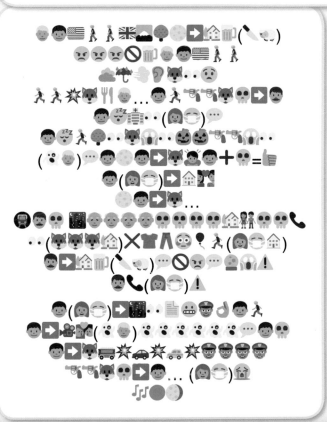

NAME THIS FILM FROM 2000.

NAME THESE FILM TITLES.

1. 1939   2. 1993   3. 1980

4. 1997   5. 1980

6. 1990   7. 2010   8. 2014

MOVIE STRINGS

NAME THESE THREE FILMS.

1. 2000   2. 1992   3. 2010

NAME THIS FILM AND ITS SEQUEL.

1. 1984   2. 1985

MOVIE STRINGS

NAME THESE THREE COEN BROTHERS FILMS.

1. 1998

2. 2007

3. 1996

MOVIE STRINGS

NAME THIS MOVIE FROM 2003.

NAME THIS MOVIE FROM 2001.

NAME THESE FILMS FROM THEIR EMOJI TITLES.

1. 2015

2. 2001

3. 1959

4. 1991

5. 1996

MOVIE STRINGS

NAME THIS MOVIE FROM 1994.

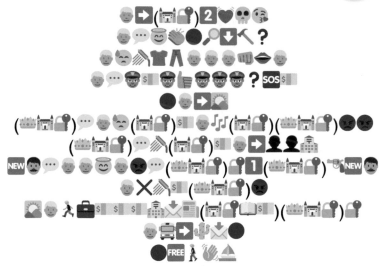

WHICH BOND FILM IS THIS?

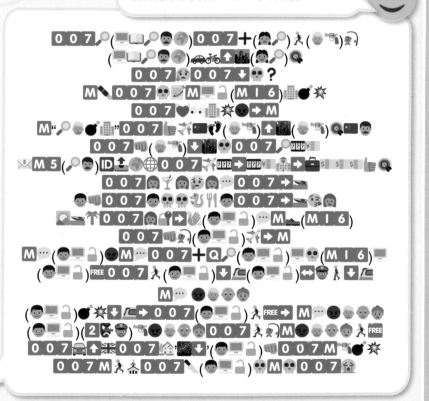

NAME THESE CLINT EASTWOOD FILMS.

1. 1964

2. 1965

3. 1966

4. 1971

5. 2004

NAME THIS HOLLYWOOD CLASSIC FROM 1939.

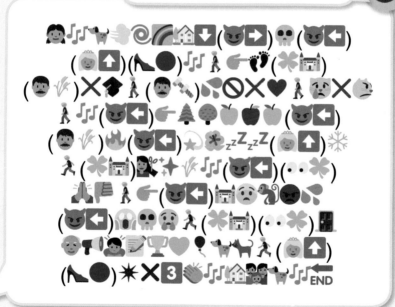

NAME THIS ROMCOM FROM 1993.

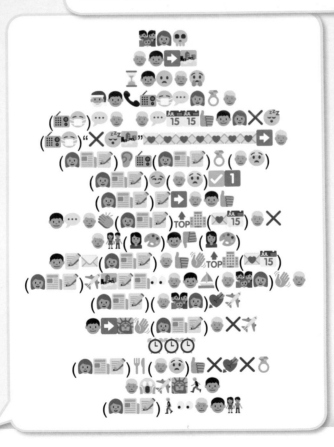

NAME THIS 2001 COMEDY.

NAME THIS 1990 FILM.

MOVIE STRINGS

WHAT FILMS ARE REPRESENTED HERE?

1. 1986   2. 1988

3. 1971   4. 1982

NAME THIS HIT MUSICAL.

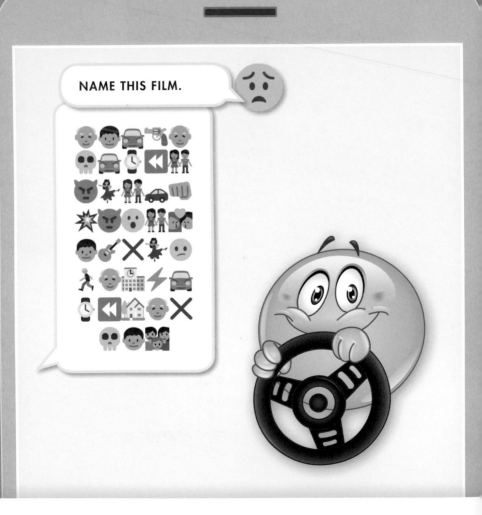

NAME THIS FILM.

NAME THIS PIXAR CLASSIC.

MOVIE STRINGS

NAME THE FAMOUS FILM QUOTES AND THE MOVIES FROM WHICH THEY COME.

1. 1942

2. 1994

3. 1979

4. 1969

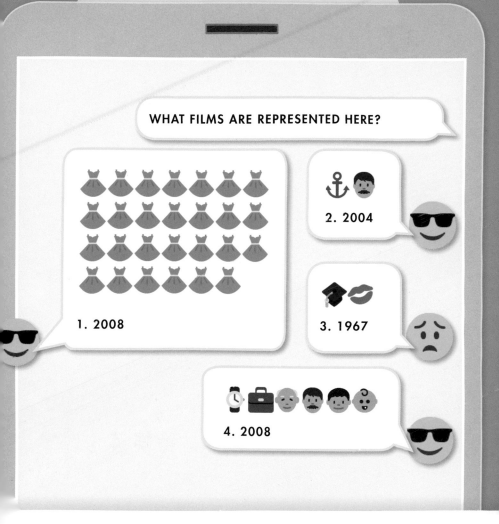

WHAT FILMS ARE REPRESENTED HERE?

1. 2008

2. 2004

3. 1967

4. 2008

MOVIE STRINGS

> **IN WHICH YEARS WERE EACH OF THE FILMS IN THIS TRILOGY RELEASED?**

1.

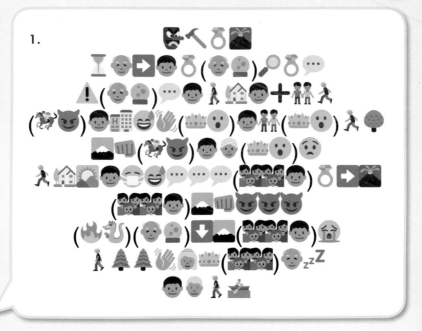

2.

3.

MOVIE STRINGS

NAME THE FILMS REPRESENTED HERE.

1. 2014

2. 1985

WHO WROTE THE BOOKS THESE FILMS WERE BASED ON? (YEAR REPRESENTS FILM'S RELEASE)

1. 2000

2. 1961

THE LITERARY EMOTICON

WHAT WAS THE WORKING TITLE FOR THIS BOOK?

NAME THESE CHILDREN'S BOOKS.

1. 🐱➡️🎩

2. 🍴1🍎2🍐3🍑4🍓5🍊 1🍰1🍦1🍌1🍔1🍕1🍭1🍒 1🐷1🎂1🍉1🍃➡️😫

NAME THIS CLASSIC.

THE LITERARY EMOTICON

WHICH CHARLES DICKENS NOVEL IS REPRESENTED HERE?

WHO IS THE AUTHOR OF THIS MODERN CHILDREN'S BESTSELLER?

THE LITERARY EMOTICON

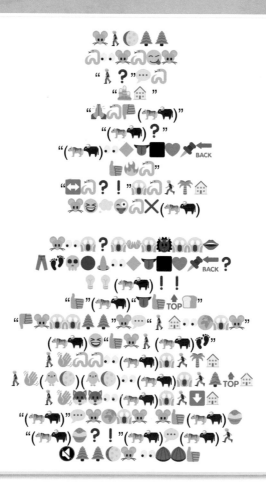

THE LITERARY EMOTICON

> **WHAT'S THIS BESTSELLING CHILDREN'S STORY?**

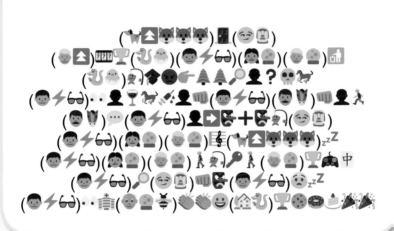

WHO WROTE THIS 18TH-CENTURY NOVEL?

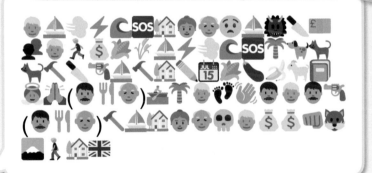

THE LITERARY EMOTICON

NAME THE TWO RIVAL PIGS FROM THIS DYSTOPIAN NOVEL.

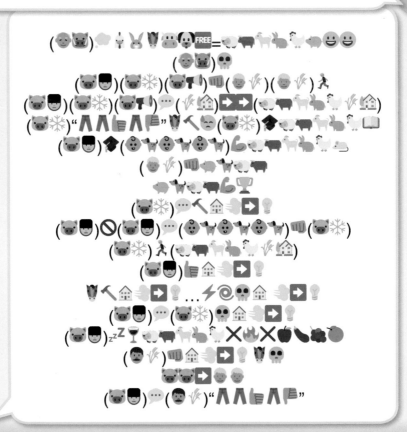

THE LITERARY EMOTICON

PUT GEORGE R. R. MARTIN'S
A SONG OF ICE AND FIRE NOVELS
IN CHRONOLOGICAL ORDER.

1.

2. (⛅🐉⚡🔪)

3. 🧚➕🐉

4.

5. 🎮(👑🪑)

6. 👑💥👑

7. 💨(⛄❄️)

THE LITERARY EMOTICON

NAME THE CHILDREN'S STORY FROM THE EMOJI PLOT.

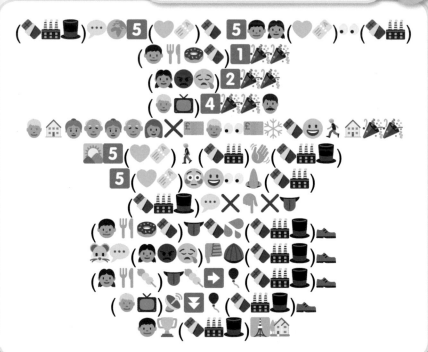

THE LITERARY EMOTICON

NAME THE 19TH-CENTURY NOVEL FROM THE QUOTE.

NAME THESE THREE NOVELS.

1. 1932   2. 1939   3. 2009

WHICH DYSTOPIAN NOVEL DOES THIS EMOJI STRING REPRESENT?

NAME THESE THREE NOVELS FROM THEIR TITLES.

1. 1962   2. 1869   3. 1960

THE LITERARY EMOTICON

> NAME THIS 19TH CENTURY FRENCH NOVEL AND ITS AUTHOR.

THE LITERARY EMOTICON

WHICH NOVELLA IS BEING REPRESENTED HERE?

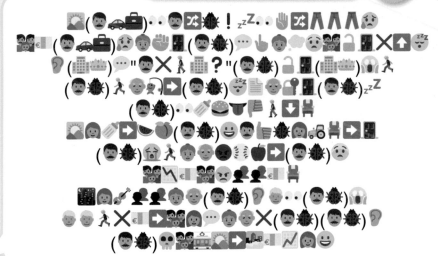

THE LITERARY EMOTICON

WHOSE ADVENTURES ARE BEING REPRESENTED HERE?

NAME THE THRILLERS FROM THEIR EMOJI TITLES.

1. 1974

2. 1934

THE LITERARY EMOTICON

NAME THE CHILDREN IN THIS CLASSIC TALE.

THE LITERARY EMOTICON

NAME THIS CHILDREN'S STORY.

WHAT YOUNG ADULT FICTION BESTSELLER IS BEING REPRESENTED HERE?

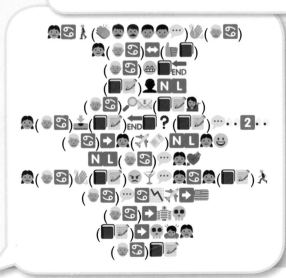

WHICH BOOKER PRIZE-WINNING NOVEL IS BEING REPRESENTED HERE?

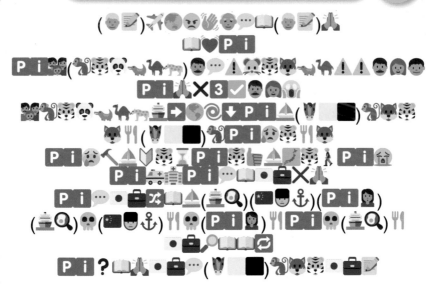

THE LITERARY EMOTICON

WHO WROTE THIS CHILDREN'S CLASSIC?

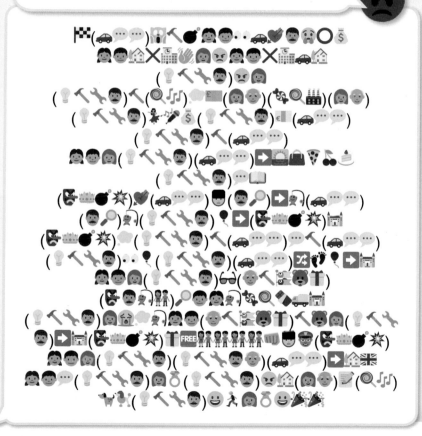

THE LITERARY EMOTICON

NAME THESE NOVELS FROM THEIR EMOJI TITLES.

1. 1908   2. 1961   3. 1939

 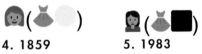

4. 1859   5. 1983

6. 1817

THE LITERARY EMOTICON

NAME THESE THREE JULES VERNE NOVELS.

1.

2.

3.

NAME THE AUTHORS OF THESE TWO 19TH-CENTURY CLASSICS.

1. 1886

2. 1844

NAME THE AUTHORS OF THESE THREE NOVELS FROM THEIR EMOJI TITLES.

1. 1945

2. 1979

3. 1960

NAME THIS FAMOUS LOVE STORY FROM 1985 AND ITS COLOMBIAN AUTHOR.

ODE TO A SMILEY

ODE TO A SMILEY

NAME THIS LYRIC POEM FIRST PUBLISHED IN 1807.

ODE TO A SMILEY

NAME THE POET RESPONSIBLE FOR THIS 17TH-CENTURY EPIC POEM.

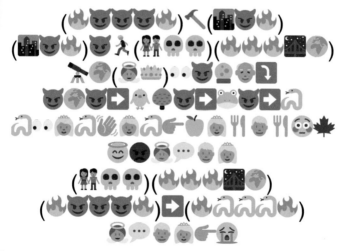

ODE TO A SMILEY

NAME THE POEM, FIRST PUBLISHED IN 1936, FROM THE LINES GIVEN HERE.

NAME THE TWO T. S. ELIOT POEMS FROM THESE EMOJI EXTRACTS.

ODE TO A SMILEY

WHAT CLASSIC NONSENSE
IS REPRESENTED HERE?

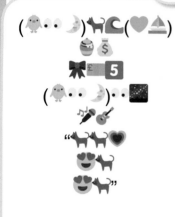

ODE TO A SMILEY

NAME THESE TWO WILLIAM BLAKE POEMS.

1.

2.

ODE TO A SMILEY

NAME THE FAMOUS AMERICAN NARRATIVE POEM AND WHO WROTE IT.

NAME THIS FAMOUS AMERICAN POEM FROM ITS FIRST LINES.

PLAYS FOR TODAY

NAME THIS ITALIAN PLAY FIRST PERFORMED IN 1921.

WHAT ABSURDIST CLASSIC IS REPRESENTED HERE?

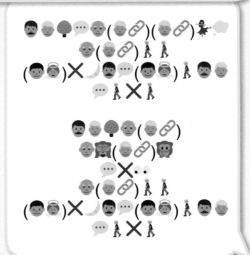

PLAYS FOR TODAY

NAME THESE THREE HENRIK IBSEN PLAYS FROM THEIR EMOJI TITLES.

1. 👘👘🏠

2. 👀👀👀

3. 👑🔨

NAME THESE THREE ANTON CHEKHOV PLAYS FROM THEIR EMOJI TITLES.

1. 🍒🌳🌳🌳

2. 👧👧👧

3. 🌊🐦

PLAYS FOR TODAY

NAME THESE TENNESSEE WILLIAMS PLAYS FROM THEIR EMOJI TITLES.

1.

2.

3.

4.

5.

PLAYS FOR TODAY

NAME THE ENGLISH PLAYWRIGHT OF THIS 16TH-CENTURY PLAY.

WHAT LATE 19TH-CENTURY PLAY IS REPRESENTED HERE?

NAME THESE PLAYS FROM THEIR EMOJI TITLES.

1. 1962

2. 2016

3. 1955

4. 1949

THE BARDICON

THE BARDICON

NAME THE SHAKESPEARE PLAY REPRESENTED HERE.

THE BARDICON

FROM WHICH PLAY IS THIS QUOTE?

FROM WHICH PLAY IS THIS STAGE DIRECTION?

THE BARDICON

IN WHICH COUNTRY IS THIS PLAY SET?

ACT 1

ACT 2

ACT 3

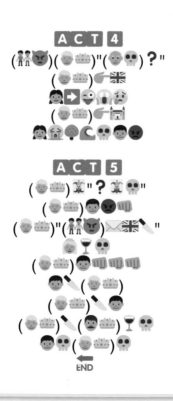

THE BARDICON

WHICH CHARACTER FROM THE PLAY BELOW IS REPRESENTED BY ?

ACT 1

ACT 2

ACT 3

THE BARDICON

WHICH PLAY'S TITLE IS REPRESENTED HERE?

NAME THE NUMBER OF THE SONNET FROM WHICH THIS QUOTE COMES.

WHICH GHOST APPEARS TO THE MAIN CHARACTER IN ACT 3 OF THIS PLAY?

ACT 1

ACT 2

ACT 3

ACT 4

ACT 5

SMILEY ON THE BOX

SMILEY ON THE BOX

NAME THESE CLASSIC US TV DRAMAS FROM THEIR TITLES...

 1.  2.   3.

4.  5.

...AND THESE FROM THEIR EMOJI SUMMARIES.

 6.

7.

SMILEY ON THE BOX

NAME THESE US TV HORROR SERIES.

1.   2.

3.

NAME THESE US ENTERTAINMENT SHOWS FROM THEIR EMOJI TITLES.

1.   2.

SMILEY ON THE BOX

WHAT AMERICAN TV COMEDY SERIES ARE REPRESENTED HERE?

1.
2.
3.
4.
5.
6.

SMILEY ON THE BOX

WHAT CLASSIC BRITISH TV SERIES ARE REPRESENTED HERE?

1. (⏳ 👑 🧴 👴) ➕ (👫 👩)(⌚ 🚀 📦)

2. 🇬🇧(🐎 👱) 👔 ☂ (💨 👩)
(🍎 👩)(👑 👩) 🔫 👊 💥 🏃 🏚

3. 👨 👴 👨🏾 💬 🚗 🚗 🚗
🚗 👤 🏁 🔂

4. (☁ ☂ ⚡) 🐤 🐥 🐧

SMILEY ON THE BOX

WHAT COSTUME DRAMA IS REPRESENTED HERE?

WHAT AMERICAN TV DRAMA SERIES ARE REPRESENTED HERE?

1.

2.

EMOJIS SING

EMOJIS SING

> **NAME THIS 1972 SONG FROM ITS EMOJI TRANSLATION.**

EMOJIS SING

NAME THIS POP SONG FROM 2010.

EMOJIS SING

NAME THIS CHRISTMAS HIT.

✖👀...✖😭...✖🙁...💬?

👲➡🏙...👲📝...👀👀...🔍😈➰😇

👲➡🏙

👲💤ᶻᶻ...👲😃...👲😈➰😇...

🐝😇4😇👍

✖👀...✖😭...✖🙁...💬?

🎅➡🏙🎅➡🏙

NAME THIS CATCHY 2013 CHORUS.

😃...👏💜🏠✖⬆TOP

😃...👏🖤😃✅

😃...👏🙆❓😃👉🧒

😃...👏💜💭👍

EMOJIS SING

NAME THIS FAMOUS SONG FIRST RELEASED IN 1971.

NAME THIS 2013 SONG.

EMOJIS SING

NAME THESE ABBA SONGS FROM THEIR EMOJI TITLES.

1.
2.
3.
4.
5.
6.

7. 🏃🏆💰💰💰
8. 👉😀👉😀👉👩 (😃⏩🕐)
9. 👩✊(zᶻᶻ💭)
10. 🎶👍👍
11. ⁉️👈👩 ⁉️👈👨
12. (🐝🧁)✖️2️⃣

13. 🐣🍴🍴🅰️
14. 👰👰👰👰👰
15. 🐑🔍❤️💕💘👩
16. ❓(👨‍👦👩)⁉️➡️

EMOJIS SING

WHICH SONG FROM A MUSICAL IS BEING REPRESENTED HERE?

NAME THE YEAR THAT THIS WAS RELEASED.

EMOJIS SING

WHAT 1968 SONG IS REPRESENTED HERE AND WHO FIRST RECORDED IT?

EMOJIS SING

WHICH 1980 CLASH SONG IS TRANSLATED HERE?

EMOJIS SING

WHICH ALBUM IS THIS THE TRACKLISTING OF?

SIDE 1

1. 💂🍕😷❤️❤️(♣️🎷🎺🎸)
2. 👶 SOS 👫
3. 👩➡️🌌➕💎💎
4. ➡️😷👍🏽
5. 🔨⚫
6. 👩🚶🏠👏
7. ➕👨📷🔥

SIDE 2

1. ➡️👱‍♀️👩➡️
2. 👦⏳6️⃣4️⃣
3. 👩🚗💷💵⏳
4. 👍🛍️🌅👍🌅
5. 💂🍕😷❤️❤️♣️(🎷🎺🎸)(⬆️)
6. 📅➡️❤️

WHAT 2011 BOYBAND HIT IS THIS?

WHAT FAMOUS CHRISTMAS CAROL IS THIS?

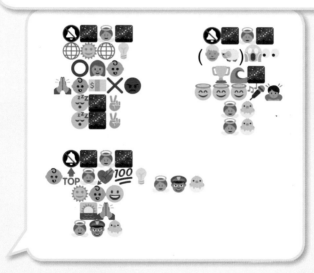

EMOJIS SING

WHICH 1990 POP SONG IS REPRESENTED BY THIS LYRIC?

WHAT ALBUM IS THIS?

NAME THESE SONGS FROM THEIR EMOJI TITLES.

1.

2.

EMOJIS SING

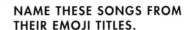

NAME THESE SONGS FROM THEIR EMOJI TITLES.

2.

1.

3.

WHICH OPERA IS THIS AND WHO WROTE IT?

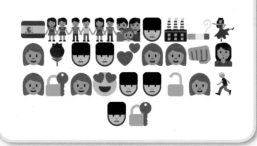

WHAT IS THIS 1954 WORLDWIDE HIT?

EMOJIS SING

NAME THIS 1978 DISCO CLASSIC.

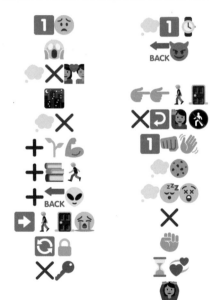

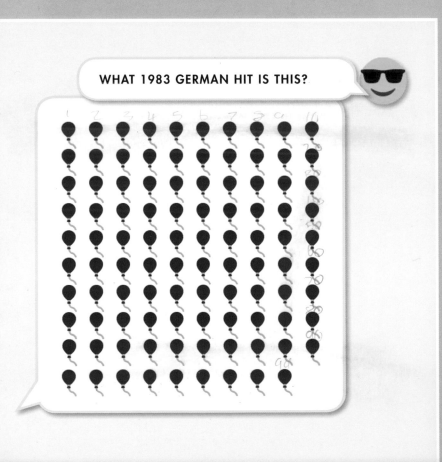

E-SPORTS

WHOSE FAMOUS ACHIEVEMENTS ARE DESCRIBED HERE IN EMOJI FORM?

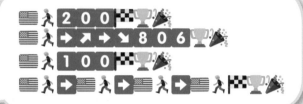

WHO'S DESCRIBING HIMSELF HERE?

💪+🦏
👊+🐋
🔗⚡
+✊↩(⚡🔊)➡(👮🏢)
💨🐱
◀📅🔪💎
⛏💎🏥💥(🏠⬜)
😡➡🔋😷

NAME THIS FAMOUS SPORTING EVENT FROM THE 1970S.

1 9 7 4 🌍 (⛵🐝) 👊 (4👨)

🔔 1 (⛵🐝) 💃 (4👨) 👊👊👊 🔔

🔔 2 (⛵🐝) 🧕👊🔍 (4👨) 👨 (4👨) 👊👊👊 🔔

🔔 3 (⛵🐝) 💬 (4👨) 😆😉 (4👨) 😠😡 (4👨) 👊👊 🔔

🔔 4 (⛵🐝) 👊 (4👨) (4👨) 🙁👿 🔔

🔔 5 (4👨) 👊 💎 (⛵🐝) 😄 (4👨) 🔔

🔔 6 (⛵🐝) 💃👤👊🔍 (4👨) 🔔

🔔 7 (4👨) 👊💎 (⛵🐝) 💬✖😄⬇? (4👨) 👿 🔔

🔔 8 (4👨) 🌧💤 (⛵🐝) 👊👊👊👊 (4👨) 📉⬇

(4👨) 🆘 " 1 2 3 4 5 6 7 8 9 " ⬆🚫 (⛵🐝) 🎉 🏆

NAME THESE SPORTSPEOPLE FROM THEIR SPORT AND NICKNAME?

1. (⚾)🅰️🐒
2. (🏀)⬛🐍
3. (🎾)🄳🃏
4. (⚽)🔶⚽⚽
5. (🏈)🍎🍹
6. (🥊)😤🐂
7. (⚾)💬👩🧒
8. (⛳)🔶🐻

AND THESE NATIONAL BASKETBALL ASSOCIATION TEAMS?

1. 🍀🍀
2. $ $
3. 🌲🐺🐺
4. 👧👧

ANSWERS

AN EMOJI HISTORY OF THE WORLD

10   The Big Bang

    The Black Death

    The discovery of the theory of gravity by Sir Isaac Newton (1687)

11   *On the Origin of Species*, Charles Darwin

    The Cold War.

12   1912 *Titanic* sinking

    Cuban Missile Crisis (1962)

13   'In the long history of the world, only a few generations have been granted the role of defending freedom in its hour of maximum danger. I do not shrink from this responsibility – I welcome it. I do not believe that any of us would exchange places with any other people or any other generation. The energy, the faith, the devotion which we bring to this endeavour will light our country and all who serve it – and the glow from that fire can truly light the world.

    And so, my fellow Americans: ask not what your country can do for you – ask what you can do for your country.' John F. Kennedy (1961)

    Julius Caesar ('I came, I saw, I conquered.')

    Moon landing (1969)

14   Boston, USA, Boston Tea Party

15   'Let them eat cake,' Marie Antoinette

    Archimedes, 'Eureka!' moment

    Copernicus came up with the theory that the Earth goes around the Sun rather than the other way round. He was from Poland.

16   The three ships were the *Niña, Pinta* and *Santa María*. Columbus discovers America

    Hannibal's. He is crossing the Alps during the Second Punic War (218–201 BCE).

WHOSE LIFE IS IT ANYWAY?

18   Elvis Presley

19   Grace Kelly

20   Catherine of Aragon, Anne Boleyn, Jane Seymour, Anne of Cleves, Catherine Howard, Catherine Parr. Henry VIII's wives

21   George Washington

22   Amy Winehouse

23   Robben Island (Nelson Mandela)

24–25   Sir Winston Churchill

    'We shall go on to the end, we shall fight in France, we shall fight on the seas and oceans, we shall fight with growing confidence and growing strength in the air, we shall defend our Island, whatever the cost may be, we shall fight on the beaches, we shall fight on the landing grounds, we shall fight in the fields and in the streets, we shall fight in the hills, we shall never surrender.'

26   Emmeline Pankhurst

    15th century (Leonardo da Vinci, b. 1452)

27   17th century (Sir Isaac Newton, b. 1643)

    19 (Joan of Arc, 1412–31)

28   Vincent van Gogh

    Crimean War, 1853–56 (Florence Nightingale)

MOVIE STRINGS

30   *Star Wars: Episode IV – A New Hope* (1977)

31   *The Godfather* (1972)

32   *The Hunger Games*

33   Harold Ramis (*Groundhog Day*)

34   *The Jungle Book* (1967)

35   *An American Werewolf in London*

36   *Billy Elliot*

37   1. *Gone with the Wind*
      2. *Alien vs. Predator*
      3. *Star Wars: Episode V – The Empire Strikes Back*
      4. *Men in Black*
      5. *The Blues Brothers*
      6. *Dances with Wolves*
      7. *The King's Speech*
      8. *Dawn of the Planet of the Apes*

38   1. *Crouching Tiger, Hidden Dragon*
      2. *Reservoir Dogs*
      3. *Eat Pray Love*

      1. *Romancing the Stone*
      2. *The Jewel of the Nile*

39   1. *The Big Lebowski*
      2. *No Country for Old Men*
      3. *Fargo*

40   *Kill Bill: Vol. 1*

      Ocean's Eleven

41   1. *Fifty Shades of Grey*
      2. *The Fast and the Furious*
      3. *Some Like It Hot*
      4. *The Silence of the Lambs*
      5. *Trainspotting*

42   *The Shawshank Redemption*

43   *Skyfall*

44   1. *A Fistful of Dollars*
      2. *For a Few Dollars More*
      3. *The Good, the Bad and the Ugly*
      4. *Dirty Harry*
      5. *Million Dollar Baby*

45   *The Wizard of Oz*

46   *Sleepless in Seattle*

47   *Zoolander*

      Pretty Woman

48   1. *Crocodile Dundee*
         ('That's not a knife... *That's* a knife!')
      2. *Big*
      3. *The French Connection*
      4. *Blade Runner*

49   *The Sound of Music*

50   *Back to the Future*

51   *WALL-E*

52   1. 'Of all the gin joints, in all the towns, in all the
         world, she had to walk into mine.' *Casablanca*
      2. 'Run Forrest, run.' *Forrest Gump*
      3. 'I love the smell of napalm in the morning.'
         Apocalypse Now
      4. 'You're only supposed to blow the bloody doors
         off!' *The Italian Job*

53   1. *27 Dresses*
      2. *Anchorman: The Legend of Ron Burgundy*
      3. *The Graduate*
      4. *The Curious Case of Benjamin Button*

54-55 1. 2001 (*The Lord of the Rings Trilogy:
         The Fellowship of the Ring*)
      2. 2002 (*The Two Towers*)
      3. 2003 (*The Return of the King*)

56   1. *Guardians of the Galaxy*
      2. *The Breakfast Club*

      1. Bret Easton Ellis (*American Psycho*)
      2. Truman Capote (*Breakfast at Tiffany's*)

THE LITERARY EMOTICON

58 First Impressions (*Pride and Prejudice* by Jane Austen)

59 1. *The Cat in the Hat* (Dr Seuss)
2. *The Very Hungry Caterpillar* (Eric Carle)

60 *The Iliad* (Homer)

61 *Oliver Twist*

62–63 Julia Donaldson (*The Gruffalo*)

64–65 *Harry Potter and the Philosopher's Stone* (J. K. Rowling)

66 Daniel Defoe (*Robinson Crusoe*)

67 *The Catcher in the Rye* (J. D. Salinger)

68 Snowball and Napoleon (*Animal Farm* by George Orwell)

69 In order:
A Game of Thrones (5)
A Clash of Kings (6)
A Storm of Swords (2)
A Feast for Crows (4)
A Dance with Dragons (3)
The Winds of Winter (7)
A Dream of Spring (1)

70 *Charlie and the Chocolate Factory* (Roald Dahl)

71 *A Tale of Two Cities* (Charles Dickens): 'It was the best of times, it was the worst of times, it was the age of wisdom, it was the age of foolishness, it was the epoch of belief, it was the epoch of incredulity, it was the season of Light, it was the season of Darkness, it was the spring of hope, it was the winter of despair.'

1. *Brave New World*, Aldous Huxley
2. *The Grapes of Wrath*, John Steinbeck
3. *Wolf Hall,* Hilary Mantel

72 *1984* (George Orwell)

1. *A Clockwork Orange* (Anthony Burgess)
2. *War and Peace* (Leo Tolstoy)
3. *To Kill a Mockingbird* (Harper Lee)

73 *Madame Bovary*, Gustave Flaubert

74 *The Metamorphosis* (Franz Kafka)

75 Sherlock Holmes

1. *Tinker Tailor Soldier Spy* (John le Carré)
2. *Murder on the Orient Express* (Agatha Christie)

76 Lucy, Edmund, Susan and Peter Pevensie (*The Lion, the Witch and the Wardrobe* by C. S. Lewis)

77 *The Tale of Peter Rabbit* (Beatrix Potter)

The Fault in Our Stars (John Green)

78 *Life of Pi* (Yann Martel)

79 Ian Fleming (*Chitty-Chitty-Bang-Bang*)

80 1. *The Wind in the Willows* (Kenneth Grahame)
2. *Catch-22* (Joseph Heller)
3. *The Big Sleep* (Raymond Chandler)
4. *The Woman in White* (Wilkie Collins)
5. *The Woman in Black* (Susan Hill)
6. *Northanger Abbey* (Jane Austen)

81 1. *Twenty Thousand Leagues Under the Sea*
2. *Around the World in Eighty Days*
3. *Journey to the Centre of the Earth*

1. Robert Louis Stevenson (*Strange Case of Dr Jekyll and Mr Hyde*)
2. Alexandre Dumas (*The Three Musketeers*)

82 1. Evelyn Waugh, *Brideshead Revisited*
2. Douglas Adams, *The Hitchhiker's Guide to the Galaxy*
3. John Updike, *Rabbit, Run*

Love in the Time of Cholera, Gabriel García Márquez

ODE TO A SMILEY

84   'I Wandered Lonely as a Cloud' ('*Daffodils*', William Wordsworth)

85   John Milton ('*Paradise Lost*')

86   '*Funeral Blues*' (W. H. Auden)

Stop all the clocks, cut off the telephone,
Prevent the dog from barking with a juicy bone,
Silence the pianos and with muffled drum
Bring out the coffin, let the mourners come.
'*The Lovesong of J. Alfred Prufrock*'

Shall I part my hair behind? Do I dare to eat a
    peach?
I shall wear white flannel trousers, and walk
    upon the beach.
I have heard the mermaids singing, each to
    each. I do not think that they will sing to me.
'*The Waste Land*'

April is the cruellest month, breeding
Lilacs out of the dead land, mixing
Memory and desire, stirring
Dull roots with spring rain.
Let aeroplanes circle moaning overhead
Scribbling on the sky the message He is Dead,
Put crêpe bows round the white necks of the
    public doves,
Let the traffic policemen wear black cotton
    gloves.
He was my North, my South, my East and West,
My working week and my Sunday rest,
My noon, my midnight, my talk, my song,
I thought that love would last forever: I was
    wrong
The stars are not wanted now, put out every one;
Pack up the moon and dismantle the sun;
Pour away the ocean and sweep up the wood.
For nothing now can ever come to any good.

87   '*The Owl and the Pussycat*' (Edward Lear)

88–89   1. '*And did those feet in ancient time*'
And did those feet in ancient time
Walk upon Englands mountains green:
And was the holy Lamb of God,
On Englands pleasant pastures seen!
And did the Countenance Divine,
Shine forth upon our clouded hills?
And was Jerusalem builded here,
Among these dark Satanic Mills?
Bring me my Bow of burning gold:
Bring me my arrows of desire:
Bring me my Spear: O clouds unfold!
Bring me my Chariot of fire!
I will not cease from Mental Fight,
Nor shall my sword sleep in my hand:
Till we have built Jerusalem,
In Englands green & pleasant Land.

2. '*The Tyger*'
Tyger Tyger, burning bright,
In the forests of the night;
What immortal hand or eye,
Could frame thy fearful symmetry?

90   '*The Raven*', Edgar Allan Poe

'*Howl*' (Allen Ginsberg)

PLAYS FOR TODAY

92	*Six Characters in Search of an Author* (Luigi Pirandello)
	Waiting for Godot (Samuel Beckett)
93	1. *A Doll's House* 2. *Ghosts* 3. *The Master Builder*
	1. *The Cherry Orchard* 2. *Three Sisters* 3. *The Seagull*
94	1. *Sweet Bird of Youth* 2. *Suddenly, Last Summer* 3. *Cat on a Hot Tin Roof* 4. *A Streetcar Named Desire* 5. *The Glass Menagerie*
95	Christopher Marlowe (*Doctor Faustus*)
96	*The Importance of Being Earnest* (Oscar Wilde) 1. *Who's Afraid of Virginia Woolf?* (Edward Albee) 2. *Harry Potter and the Cursed Child* (J. K. Rowling, Jack Thorne and John Tiffany) 3. *A View from the Bridge* (Arthur Miller) 4. *Death of a Salesman* (Arthur Miller)

THE BARDICON

98	*King Lear*
99	*As You Like It*: 'All the world's a stage, And all the men and women merely players; They have their exits and their entrances, And one man in his time plays many parts, His acts being seven ages.
	At first the infant, Mewling and puking in the nurse's arms; And then the whining school-boy, with his satchel; And shining morning face, creeping like snail; Unwillingly to school. And then the lover, Sighing like furnace, with a woeful ballad; Made to his mistress' eyebrow. Then a soldier, Full of strange oaths, and bearded like the pard, Jealous in honour, sudden and quick in quarrel, Seeking the bubble reputation; Even in the cannon's mouth. And then the justice, In fair round belly with good capon lin'd, With eyes severe and beard of formal cut, Full of wise saws and modern instances; And so he plays his part. The sixth age shifts; Into the lean and slipper'd pantaloon, With spectacles on nose and pouch on side; His youthful hose, well sav'd, a world too wide; For his shrunk shank; and his big manly voice, Turning again toward childish treble, pipes; And whistles in his sound. Last scene of all, That ends this strange eventful history, Is second childishness and mere oblivion; Sans teeth, sans eyes, sans taste, sans everything.
	The Winter's Tale: 'Exit, pursued by a bear'
100–101	Denmark (*Hamlet*)
102–103	Paris (*Romeo and Juliet*)
	A Midsummer Night's Dream
	'*Sonnet 18*': 'Shall I compare thee to a summer's day?
104	Banquo (*Macbeth*)

SMILEY ON THE BOX

106
1. *Mad Men*
2. *One Tree Hill*
3. *Deadwood*
4. *Orange is the New Black*
5. *House of Cards*
6. *Lost*
7. *House*

107
1. *American Horror Story*
2. *The Walking Dead*
3. *Hannibal*

1. *The Price is Right*
2. *America's Next Top Model*

108
1. *Friends*
2. *Happy Days*
3. *Cheers*
4. *Arrested Development*
5. *The Fresh Prince of Bel-Air*
6. *Sex and the City*

109
1. *Doctor Who*
2. *The Avengers*
3. *Top Gear*
4. *Thunderbirds*

110 *Downton Abbey*
1. *Twin Peaks*
2. *The X-Files*

EMOJIS SING

112 'Crocodile Rock' (Elton John)

113 'Firework' (Katy Perry)

114 'Santa Claus is Coming to Town' (Various)

'Happy' (Pharrell Williams)

115 'Imagine' (John Lennon)

116 'Let it Go' (Idina Menzel)

117
1. *'Dancing Queen'*
2. *'Money, Money, Money'*
3. *'Summer Night City'*
4. *'Waterloo'*
5. *'Angel Eyes'*
6. *'Ring Ring'*
7. *'The Winner Takes it All'*
8. *'Gimme! Gimme! Gimme!'*
9. *'I Have a Dream'*
10. *'Thank You for the Music'*
11. *'Knowing Me Knowing You'*
12. *'Honey, Honey'*
13. *'Chiquitita'*
14. *'I Do, I Do, I Do, I Do'*
15. *'Lay All Your Love on Me'*
16. *'Does Your Mother Know'*

118 'Do You Hear the People Sing?' from *Les Misérables*

1970 ('ABC', The Jackson 5)

119 '(Sittin' On) The Dock of the Bay', Otis Redding

120 'Bankrobber'

121 *Sgt. Pepper's Lonely Hearts Club Band* (The Beatles)

Side 1:
1. *'Sgt. Pepper's Lonely Hearts Club Band'*
2. *'With a Little Help from My Friends'*
3. *'Lucy in the Sky with Diamonds'*
4. *'Getting Better'*
5. *'Fixing a Hole'*
6. *'She's Leaving Home'*
7. *'Being for the Benefit of Mr. Kite!'*

Side 2:
1. 'Within You Without You'
2. 'When I'm Sixty-Four'
3. 'Lovely Rita'
4. 'Good Morning Good Morning'
5. 'Sgt. Pepper's Lonely Hearts Club Band (Reprise)'
6. 'A Day in the Life'

122 'Gotta Be You' (One Direction)

123 'Silent Night'

124 'U Can't Touch This' (MC Hammer, 'Stop, Hammer time!')

OK Computer (Radiohead)

1. 'Bridge Over Troubled Water' (Simon & Garfunkel)

2. 'I Heard it Through the Grapevine' (Various)

125 1. 'Twinkle, Twinkle, Little Star'
2. 'Unchained Melody' (Various)
3. 'The House of the Rising Sun' (Various)

126 *Carmen*, Georges Bizet

127 'Rock Around the Clock' (Bill Haley & His Comets)

128 'I Will Survive' (Gloria Gaynor)

129 Scissor Sisters

Don Henley ('The Boys of Summer')

130 '99 Red Balloons' (Nena)

E-SPORTS

132 Jesse Owens

Muhammad Ali:
'I've wrestled with alligators,
I've tussled with a whale.
I done handcuffed lightning
And throw thunder in jail.
You know I'm bad.
Just last week, I murdered a rock,
Injured a stone, hospitalized a brick.
I'm so mean, I make medicine sick.'

133 The Rumble in the Jungle (George Foreman vs. Muhammad Ali, 1974)

134 1. Manchester United F.C. (Red Devils)
2. Ajax Amsterdam (Sons of Gods)
3. Juventus F.C. (The Old Lady)
4. England national football team (Three Lions)

1. Arizona Diamondbacks
2. Chicago Cubs
3. Minnesota Twins
4. Toronto Blue Jays

135 1. Alex Rodriguez ('A-Rod', baseball)
2. Kobe Bryant ('Black Mamba', basketball)
3. Novak Djokovic ('Djoker', tennis)
4. David Beckham ('Goldenballs', football)
5. O. J. Simpson ('OJ', American football)
6. Jack LaMotta ('The Raging Bull', boxing)
7. Willie Mays ('The Say Hey Kid', baseball)
8. Jack Nicklaus ('The Golden Bear', golf)

1. Boston Celtics
2. Milwaukee Bucks
3. Minnesota Timberwolves
4. Los Angeles Clippers

136 Carl Lewis